KEYBOARD ACCOMPANIMENT
GRADE 6

Scott Foresman

Editorial Offices: Parsippany, New Jersey • Glenview, Illinois • New York, New York
Sales Offices: Parsippany, New Jersey • Duluth, Georgia • Glenview, Illinois
Carrollton, Texas • Ontario, California

ISBN: 0-382-34489-8

Contents

To the Teacher

Keyboard accompaniments are provided for those songs for which the keyboard is an appropriate instrument or a reasonable substitute for authentic instruments.

The triangle-shaped boxes within an accompaniment designate the beginnings of lines of music on the student page. Harmonies in an accompaniment may differ from those on the recording and from the chord symbols in the student text.

Your Life Is Now

Words and Music by
John Mellencamp and George M. Green
Arranged by Buddy Skipper

VERSE

1. See the moon___ roll___ a - cross___ the stars,___
2. Would you teach your chil – dren to tell the truth?___

See the sea-sons turn___ like a heart.___
Would you take the high___ road if you could choose?___

Your fa-ther's days are lost___ to___
Do you be - lieve you're a vic - tim___ of a great com-pro-

you,___ / mise?

This is___ your time___ here___ to do___
'Cause I be-lieve___ you___ could change your___ mind___

___ what you will do.___ / ___ and change our___ lives.___

REFRAIN

Your life___ is now, your life___ is now,___

___ your life___ is now.___

In this un - dis-cov-ered mo-

ment___ lift your head up a-bove the crowd;___ we could shake___

4

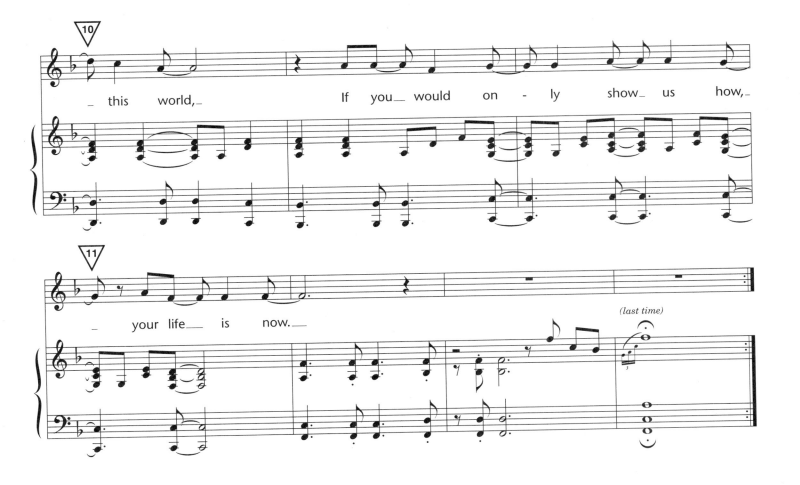

this world,___ If you___ would on - ly show___ us how,___

your life___ is now.___

(last time)

A Brand New Day

Words and Music by Luther Vandross
Arranged by Ting Ho

Driving

REFRAIN

Can't you___ feel a___ brand new___ day?___

(Last time, repeat ad lib)

Can't you___ feel a___ brand new___ day?___

5

Bury Me Not on the Lone Prairie

Cowboy Song from the United States
Arranged by Georgette LeNorth

Red River Valley

Cowboy Song from the United States
Arranged by Buddy Skipper

Bắt kim thang (Setting Up the Golden Ladder)

English Words by Alice Firgau

Traditional Song from Vietnam
Arranged by Ting Ho

Steadily

Bắt kim thang cà lang bí__ rồ. Cột qua kèo kèo qua
Set the gold - en lad - der__ up; Now jump left, then jump

cột. Chú bán đầu qua cầu mà té. Chú bán ếch ở lại làm
right. What a sight! A ven - dor falls from the bridge; an - oth - er

chi. Con le le đánh trống thổi__ kèn. Con bìm
calls. The le le bird plays trum - pet and drum, And the

bịp thổi tò tí te tò te.__
bim bip bird sings te twiddle dee dum.__

Lean on Me

Words and Music by Bill Withers
Arranged by Mollye Otis

VERSE

1. Some - times in our lives___ we all have pain,___ we all have
2. Please swal-low your pride___ if I have things___ you need to
3. If there is a load___ you have to bear___ that you can't

sor - row.___ But if we are wise___ we know that there's___
bor - row,___ For no one can fill___ those of your needs___
car - ry,___ I'm right up the road.___ I'll share your load___

al - ways to - mor - row.
that you won't let_____ show.
if you just call_____ me.

Lean on me_____ when you're not strong_

and I'll be your friend,_ I'll help you car - ry on,_

Last time to Coda ⊕

For it won't be long_ till I'm gon - na need_ some - bod - y to lean_

on.__ _____ on.__ Just call on me, broth-er, when

you need a hand.__ We all__ need some-bod-y to lean_____ on. I just

might have a prob-lem that you'd un-der-stand.__ We all__ need some-bod-y to lean__

Magnolia

Words and Music by Tish Hinojosa
Arranged by Joyce Kalbach

1. Tem - pra - no en la ma - ña - na un pa - ja - ri - to can - ta, des
2. Ve - ra - no se a - ca - ba tam - bién el jue - go pa - ra,
1. Ear - ly in the morn - ing, I can hear the birds sing,
2. Sum - mer - time is end - ing, ain't no more pre - tend - ing,

pier - ta la mag - no - li - a.
ba - jo la mag - no - li - a.
un - der the mag - no - lia tree.
un - der the mag - no - lia tree.

Su can - ción me ha - bla,
Ho - jas caen de o - to - ño,
When I hear it sweet - ly,
Au - tumn leaves are fall - ing,

dul - ce y tan cla - ra,
a - nun - cian - do in - vier - no,
I am there com - plete - ly,
win - ter - time is call - ing,

ba - jo la mag - no - li - a.
ba - jo la mag - no - li - a.
un - der the mag - no - lia tree.
un - der the mag - no - lia tree.

Flor blan - ca y bo - ni - ta
Mi her - ma - ni - ta y yo con
Blos - soms big and white, and
My sis - ter and me, we

ho - jas bien bri - lla - das,
té y de - sa - yu - no,
leaves so big and shin - y,
sit and have some tea here,

cre - cen en mag - no - li -
ba - ja la mag - no - li -
grow on the mag - no - lia
un - der the mag - no - lia

15

Gonna Build a Mountain

Words and Music by Leslie Bricusse and Anthony Newley
Arranged by Georgette LeNorth

Put On a Happy Face

Words by Lee Adams

Music by Charles Strouse
Arranged by James Rooker

Gray skies are gon-na clear up,____ put on a hap-py face;

Brush off the clouds and cheer up,____ put on a hap-py face.

Take off the gloom-y mask of trag - e-dy, it's not your style;

You'll look so good that you'll be glad ya' de - cid-ed to smile!

Pick out a pleas-ant out - look, stick out that no - ble chin;

Wipe off that "full of doubt" look,_____ slap on a hap-py grin! And

spread sun-shine all o-ver the place, Just put on a

hap - py face!

face!_____

Adiós, Amigos (Goodbye, My Friends)

English Words by Donald Scafuri

Folk Song from New Mexico
Arranged by Carol Jay

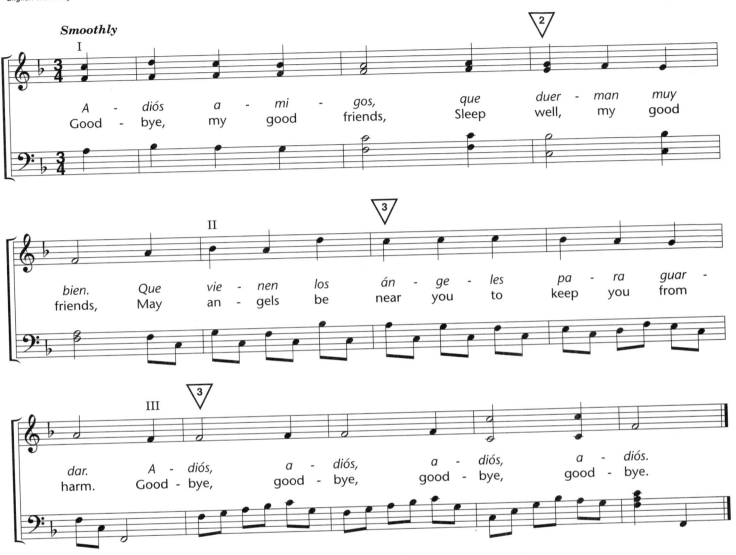

La mariposa (The Butterfly)

English Words by Aura Kontra

Folk Song from Bolivia
Arranged by Alan Seale

Strong

La la la la lai   la lai   la lai   la lai lai   lai lai lai,

2

La la la la lai   la lai   la lai   la lai   la la la la   lai   lai lai.

3

Al   son de las   ma - tra - cas   to - dos can - tan   y bai - lan
Hear   the rat - tles'   rhyth - mic beat,   Call - ing us   to   sing   and dance

4

La   mo - re - na - da   Con   las   pal - mas,
to   the live - ly   sound.   Clap   your   hands   now,   *(clap)*

con   los   ta - cos.   *(stamp)*
kick   your heels   up,

¡Vi - va la fies - ta!
turn   your part - ner 'round.

¡Vi - va la fies - ta!
Turn   your part - ner 'round,

¡Vi - va la fies - ta!   *(clap)*
turn   your part - ner 'round.

Yü guang guang (Moonlight Lullaby)

English Words by Aura Kontra

Folk Song from Hong Kong
As Sung by Shin-Pai Li
Arranged by Alice Firgau

ah   yeh   tai ngow   koy   tsü(ng)_____ sahn_____ gong_____
your   grand - fa - ther   will   watch_____ the   cat-tle_____ a -
your   grand - fa - ther   needs   you   to watch the   cat-tle_____ a -

graz   -   ing on   the   hill.
graz   -   ing on   the   hill.

Wai bamba

Shona Wedding Song
Arranged by Carol Jay

Hey, Ho! Nobody Home

Old English Round
Arranged by Buddy Skipper

Rock and Roll Is Here to Stay

Words and Music by David White
Arranged by Carol Jay

We don't care what peo-ple say,   Rock and roll is here to stay.
Rock and roll will al-ways be,   It'll go down in his-to-ry.
We don't care what peo-ple say,   Rock and roll is here to stay.

REFRAIN

Ev - 'ry - bod - y rock,   Ev - 'ry - bod - y rock,

Ev - 'ry - bod - y rock,   Ev - 'ry - bod - y rock,

Come   on,   ev - 'ry - bod - y   rock and roll.

Give My Regards to Broadway

Words and Music by George M. Cohan
Arranged by Carol Jay

I will soon be there;_____ Whis-per of how I'm yearn -

ing to min-gle with the old - time throng,_____ Give my re -

gards to old Broad-way and say that I'll be there ere long._____

Farewell to Tarwathie

Folk Song from Scotland
Arranged by Ian Linn

1. Fare - well to Tar - wa - thie, A - dieu Mor-mond Hill, And the dear land of
2. Fare - well to my com - rades for a - while I must part, And_ like - wise the

Crim - mond I bid thee fare - well. I'm bound out for Green-land and
dear lass who first won my heart, The cold coast of Green-land my

read - y to sail, In_ hopes to find rich - es in hunt-ing the whale.
heart will not chill, The_ long - er the ab-sence the more lov-ing she'll feel.

3. Our ship is well rigged, and she's ready to sail,
   The crew, they are anxious to follow the whale.
   Where the icebergs do float and the stormy winds blow,
   Where the land and the ocean is covered with snow.

4. The cold coast of Greenland is barren and bare,
   No seedling nor harvest is ever known there,
   And the birds here sing sweetly in mountain and vale,
   But there's no bird in Greenland to sing to the whale.

Barb'ry Allen

Folk Song from the British Isles
Arranged by Ian Linn

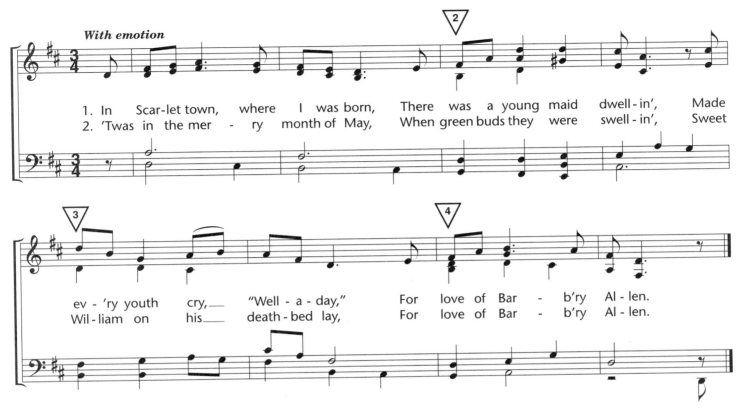

1. In Scar-let town, where I was born, There was a young maid dwell-in', Made
2. 'Twas in the mer - ry month of May, When green buds they were swell-in', Sweet

ev - 'ry youth cry,___ "Well - a - day," For love of Bar - b'ry Al - len.
Wil - liam on his___ death - bed lay, For love of Bar - b'ry Al - len.

3. He sent his servant to the town,
   To the place where she was dwellin',
   Cried, "Master bids you come to him,
   If your name be Barb'ry Allen."

4. Then slowly, slowly she got up,
   And slowly went she nigh him,
   And when she pulled the curtains back
   Said, "Young man, I think you're dyin'."

5. "Oh, yes, I'm sick, I'm very sick,
   And I never will be better,
   Until I have the love of one,
   The love of Barb'ry Allen."

6. Then lightly tripped she down the stairs,
   She trembled like an aspen.
   "'Tis vain, 'tis vain, my dear young man,
   To long for Barb'ry Allen."

7. She walked out in the green, green fields,
   She heard his death bells knellin'.
   And every stroke they seemed to say,
   "Hard-hearted Barb'ry Allen."

8. "Oh, father, father, dig my grave,
   Go dig it deep and narrow.
   Sweet William died for me today;
   I'll die for him tomorrow."

9. They buried her in the old churchyard,
   Sweet William's grave was nigh her,
   And from his heart grew a red, red rose,
   And from her heart a brier.

10. They grew and grew o'er the old church wall,
    'Till they could grow no higher,
    Until they tied a lover's knot,
    The red rose and the brier.

My Dear Companion

Words and Music by Jean Ritchie
Arranged by Buryl Red
Piano accompaniment by John Girt

Oh, have you seen my dear com-pan-ion,

for he was all this world to me. I hear he's
(she) (she's)

gone to some far coun-try, and that he cares
(she)

no more for_ me.   I wish I were   some swal-low

fly - in',   I'd fly to a high   and lone-some place.

There, join the_ wild   birds in their cry-in',   Re - member-ing_

you   and your sweet_ face. (sweet   face.)

35

El condor pasa

English words by Aura Kontra

Music by Daniel Almonica Robles
Arranged by Mollye Otis

ras,
be

más pien - so que no vi - vi - ré co - mo po -
when it has flown back whence it came. I do not

dré.
know.

Mmm
Mmm

mp

decresc.

rall.

Greensleeves

Folk Song from England
Arranged by Bernard Heiden

39

Glory, Glory, Hallelujah

Traditional Gospel Song
Arranged by Georgette LeNorth

Scarborough Fair

Folk Song from England
Arranged by James Roberts

Harrison Town

Folk Song from the Ozarks
Adapted by Jill Trinka
Arranged by Jill Gallina

1. Come, all you ram-blin', scram-blin' boys, where-ev-er you may be, And
2. As I went out from Harris-on Town a couple of days a-go, I

lis-ten to my sto-ry, and shun bad com-pa-ny, I
turned my face to-ward the west, to Eu-re-ka I did go, Well the

know I've been a cu-ri-ous lad and you know my ev-'ry flaw, But
Harris-on crowd that fol-lowed me, they knew I'd have no doubt, That

I'll step out to hear them shout for me in Ar-kan-sas.
I'd be back in Berry-ville be-fore the week was out.

What a Wonderful World

Music and Words by George David Weiss and Bob Thiele
Arranged by John Girt

world.　　　　　　　　　　　　　　The　col-ors of the rain-bow,　so

pret-ty in the sky,　are al-so on the fac-es　of peo-ple go-in' by,　I see

friends shak-in' hands,＿ say-in', "How　do you do?"　They're real-ly say-in',

rall.　　　　　　　　*a tempo*
"I　love you." I hear ba - bies cry,　I watch them grow,

Sing a Song of Peace

"This Is My Country" – Words by Don Ray

Music by Al Jacobs
Words and Arrangement by Jill Gallina

With great feeling

Sing a song of peace through the world, till ev-'ry land is sing - ing.

This is my coun - try, land of my birth;

Sound the bells of peace through the world, with ev-'ry na - tion ring - ing.

This is my coun - try, grand - est on earth.

Don't Cry for Me, Argentina

Words by Tim Rice

Music by Andrew Lloyd Webber
Arranged by Buddy Skipper

With deep emotion

Tempo rubato

It won't be ea-sy, you'll think it strange when I try____ to ex-plain____ how I feel, That I still need your love af-ter all____ that I've done,____

48

run - ning a - round,_____ try - ing ev - 'ry - thing new, but the
not the so - lu - tions they prom - ised to be, the

noth - ing im - pressed me at all, I nev - er ex - pect - ed it
an - swer was here all the time, I love you, and hope you love

REFRAIN

to. Don't cry for me, Ar - gen - ti - na, the
me.

truth is I nev-er left you.___ All through my wild days, my mad ex-

is-tence,___ I kept my prom-ise,___ don't keep your

dis-tance.___

dis-tance.___

Repeat Refrain

I Walk the Unfrequented Road

Words by Frederick L. Hosmer

Folk Hymn from the United States
Arranged by Paul Somers

Do, Re, Mi, Fa

The School Round Book, 1852
Arranged by Alice Firgau

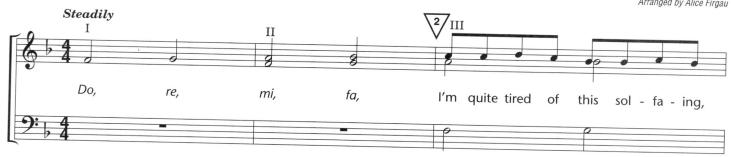

Do, re, mi, fa, I'm quite tired of this sol - fa - ing,

I've for - got all you've been say - ing. Do, re, mi, fa,

I'm quite tired of this sol - fa - ing, I've for - got all you've been say - ing.

Do, re, mi, fa, Do.

Do, Re, Mi, Fa (Alternate Accompaniment)

The School Round Book, 1852
Arranged by Alice Firgau

Hava nashira

Round from Israel
Arranged by Judith C. Lane

Ain't Gonna Let Nobody Turn Me 'Round

African American Civil Rights Song
Arranged by John Girt

keep on   a - talk - in',   March-in' to the free - dom land.___

Bridges *The accompaniment for this song is found on p. 60.*

Blue Skies

Words and Music by Irving Berlin
Arranged by Marilyn J. Patterson

Bridges

Words and Music by Bill Staines
Arranged by Mark A. Miller

Sincerely

1. There are bridg-es, bridg-es in the sky, They are shin-ing in the sun.___ They are
2. There are can-yons, there are can-yons. They are yawn-ing in the night.___ They are
3. Let us build a bridge of mu-sic, Let us cross it with a song.___ Let us

stone and steel and wood and wire, They can change two things to one.___ They are
rank and bit-ter an-ger, They are all de-void of light.___ They are
span an-oth-er can-yon, Let us right an-oth-er wrong.___ And if

lan-guag-es and let-ters, They are po-et-ry and all.___ They are
fear and blind sus-pi-cion, They are ap-a-thy and pride,_ They are
some-one should ask us Where we're off and bound to-day,___ We will

love and un-der-stand-ing,___ And they're bet-ter than a wall.___
dark and so fore-bod-ing,___ And they're oh, so ver-y wide.___
tell them "build-ing bridg-es,"___ And be off and on our way.___

Birthday

Words and Music by John Lennon and Paul McCartney
Arranged by Buddy Skipper

I'm glad it's your birth - day, ___ Hap-py

birth-day to ___ you. ___

Yes, we're go - in' to a par - ty, par - ty, ___ Yes, we're go-in' to a

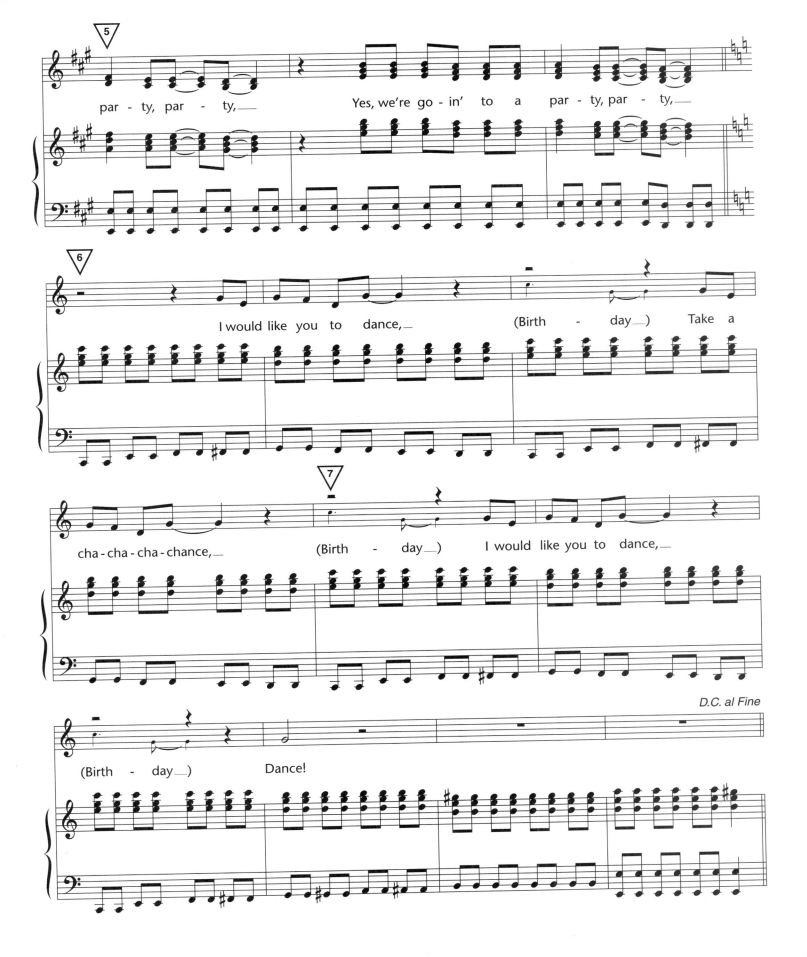

I Got Rhythm

Words by Ira Gershwin

Music by George Gershwin
Arranged by Arnold Siegel

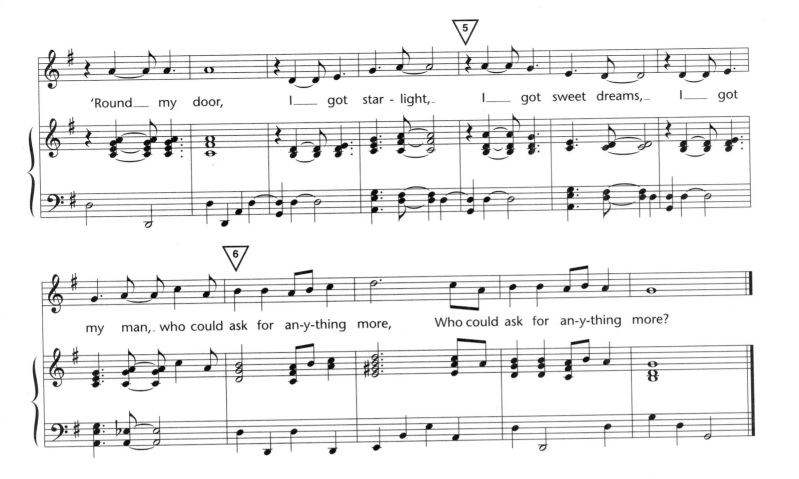

'Round__ my door, I__ got star - light,_ I__ got sweet dreams,_ I__ got

my man,_ who could ask for an-y-thing more, Who could ask for an-y-thing more?

Music Goes with Anything

Words and Music by Sarah and Robert Sterling
Arranged by Don Kalbach

(Note: Some of the repeats indicated in the Student Edition are fully notated in this accompaniment.)

goes!

4 VERSE

1. What wakes me up in the mornin'?

5

What bright-ens up my drea-ry day?___ What grabs my

6

heart with-out a warn-in' and takes it up, up and a-way?___

7

Bar-ber-shop, jazz, rock, op-'ra, and dis-co, all have a

charm that en - thralls._ They left my heart in San Fran - cis - co, in

Par - is, and in Mon - te - zu - ma's halls! Don' - cha know that

REFRAIN

Mu - sic keeps me snap - pin' my fin - gers. Mu - sic keeps me

Countermelody 1

Mu - sic,_ I love mu - sic,_

tap-pin' my toes.___ Mu - sic goes with an - y - thing,___ and with

me an' my mu - sic.___

1.

mu - sic, an - y - thing goes!

2.

mu - sic, an - y - thing

Why don't you sing a - long some

Why don't you

goes!

VERSE

2. Rag - time! Two good beats an' I'm danc - in',

sing a - long.

Sou - sa has me march-in' right a - long! Gil - bert and Sul - li - van

are en - tranc - in'. Dick an' Os - car got me sing-in' their songs!

REFRAIN

Don' - cha know that Mu - sic keeps me snap-pin' my fin - gers.

Countermelody 2

1. So the day is dark and gloom - y,
2. So my jokes just aren't that fun - ny,

music, _____ an-y-thing goes! _____

music, _____ an-y-thing goes! _____

Student Page 112

Hit Me with a Hot Note and Watch Me Bounce

Words by Don George

Music by Duke Ellington
Arranged by Buddy Skipper

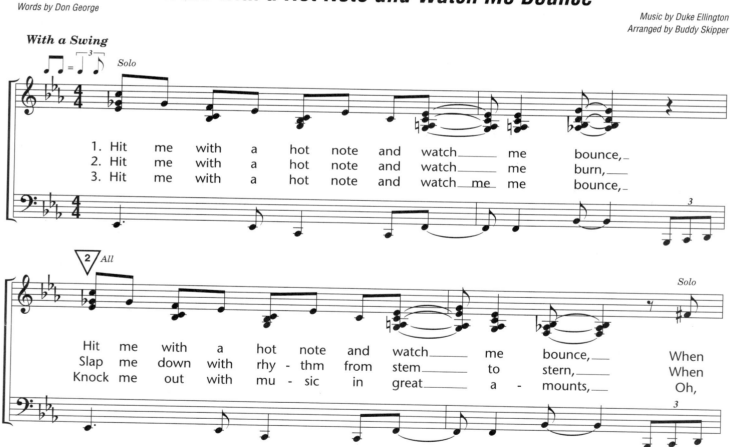

With a Swing

Solo

1. Hit   me   with   a   hot   note   and   watch_____ me   bounce,_
2. Hit   me   with   a   hot   note   and   watch_____ me   burn,_____
3. Hit   me   with   a   hot   note   and   watch__me   me   bounce,_

2 All

Solo

Hit   me   with   a   hot   note   and   watch_____ me   bounce,_____ When
Slap me   down   with   rhy - thm   from   stem_____ to   stern,_____ When
Knock me   out   with   mu - sic   in   great_____ a - mounts,___ Oh,

At the Same Time

Words and Music by Ann Hampton Callaway
Arranged by Carol Jay

When it comes to think-ing of to-mor-row,_____ we must pro-tect our__ frag-ile des - ti-

ny. In__ this pre-cious life,__ there's no time to bor-row__ The

time has come to be__ a fam-i - ly_____ Oh,__

D.S. (go to 3rd ending) al Coda

Coda

build a world__ that loves and un-der - stands,_____ It helps to

think of all___ the hearts   beat-ing in the world___   and hope for all___ the hearts___

beat-ing   in   the world. There's a heal-ing   mu-sic   in   our   hearts,_____

beat-ing in this world   at the same   time,   at the

same_____   time.

Blue Mountain Lake

Adapted by Susan Brumfield

Lumberjack Song from New York
Arranged by David Eddleman

A moderate swing

1. Come, all you good fel-lers wher - ev - er you be. Come,
2. There's the Sul - li - van bro-thers and Big Jim-my Lou, And
3. And now, my good fel-lers, a - dieu to you all, For

set down a while and lis-ten to me. The truth, I will tell you with -
old Mose Gil-bert and Dan-dy Pat, too. A lot of good fel-lers as
Christ-mas is com-ing, I'm going to Glen Falls. And when I get there, I'll go

out a mis-take, Of the rack - ets we had a - round
ev - er were seen, And they all worked for Grif - fin on
out on a spree, For you know when I've mon - ey, there's

Blue Moun-tain Lake. Der - ry down, down, down, der - ry down.
town-ship nine-teen. Der - ry down, down, down, der - ry down.
no hold-ion' me! Der - ry down, down, down, der - ry down.

Swanee

Words by Irving Caesar

Music by George Gershwin
Arranged by John Evanston

4 Down by the Swa - nee.____ The folks up north will

5 see me no more____ When I get to that Swa - nee shore.____

One Morning in May

Folk Song from the Appalachian Mountains
Arranged by Judith C. Lane

1. One morn-ing, one morn-ing, one morn-ing in May, I
morn-ing, good morn-ing, good morn-ing to thee, Oh

met a fair cou-ple a-mak-ing their way, And one was a maid-en so
where are you go-ing my pret-ty la-dy?" "O I am a-go-ing to the

bright and so fair, And the oth-er was a sol-dier and a brave vol-un-teer.
banks of the sea, To___ see the wa-ters glid-ing, hear the night-in-gale sing."

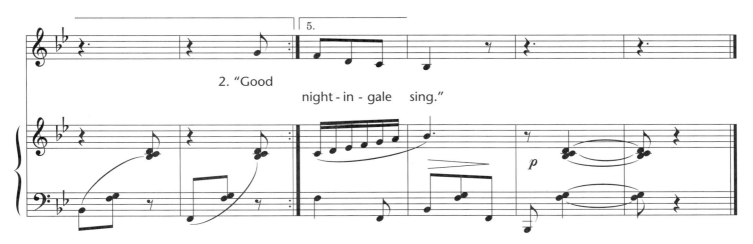

2. "Good night - in - gale sing."

3. We hadn't been standing but a minute or two,
   When out from his knapsack a fiddle he drew,
   And the tune that he played made the valleys all ring,
   Oh, see the waters gliding, hear the nightingale sing.

4. "Pretty soldier, pretty soldier, will you marry me?"
   "Oh, no, pretty lady, that never can be;
   I've a wife in old London and children twice three;
   Two wives and the army's too many for me."

5. "I'll go back to London and stay there one year,
   And often I'll think of you, my little dear,
   If ever I return, 'twill be in the spring
   To see the waters gliding, hear the nightingale sing."

Student Page 124

Dance for the Nations

Words and Music by John Krumm
Arranged by John Girt

'Round and 'round we turn, we hold___ each oth-ers' hands, And weave our -

selves in a cir - cle. The time is gone, the dance goes_ on.

Catch a Falling Star

Words and Music by Paul Vance and Lee Pockriss
Arranged by Ian Willaims

Alleluia

Music by Wolfgang Amadeus Mozart
Arranged by Alice Firgau

Strike Up the Band

Words by Ira Gershwin

Music by George Gershwin
Arranged by Marilyn J. Patterson

With excitement

Let the drums roll out!_____ Let the trum-pet call!_____ While the peo-ple shout!___ Strike up the band!_____ Hear the cym-bals ring!_____ Call-ing

one and all_____ to the mar-tial swing._____ Strike up the band!_____

Yan - kee Doo, Doo-dle-oo, Doo-dle - oo, We'll come through, Doo-dle-oo, Doo-dle -

oo, For the Red, White and Blue, Doo - dle - oo, Lend a hand!_____

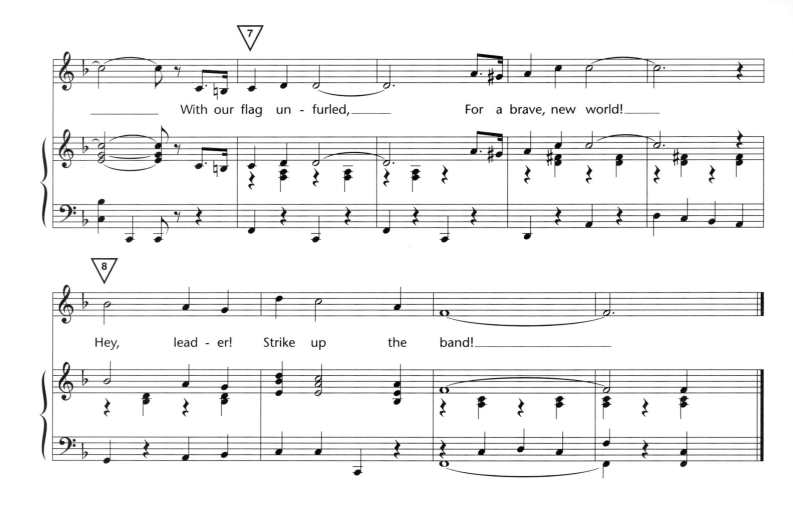

Alexander's Ragtime Band

Words and Music by Irving Berlin
Arranged by Carmen Culp and Don Kalbach

come on and hear, It's the best band in the land.

hear, It's the best band in the land. They can

Play like you nev - er heard be-fore, So you'll

play a bu - gle call like you nev - er heard be-fore, So nat - u - ral that you'll

ask for more; It's the best band in the

al - ways ask for more; It's the best band in the

Give a Little Love

Words and Music by Al Hammond and Diane Warren
Arranged by Ned Ginsburg

How to make a bright - er day,___   What do___ we do?
We can learn to make it right.___   What do___ we do?

REFRAIN

We got to give a lit - tle love,   have___ a lit - tle hope,   make___

___ this world a lit - tle bet - ter.   Try a lit - tle more,   hard -

er than be - fore, let's do what we can do to - geth - er.   Oh -

whoah - oh,___ We can ev - en make it bet -

ter, yeah.___ Oh - whoah,___ la, la, la, On - ly if we try.___

(last time repeat refrain ad lib)

We got to ___ If ev - 'ry -

bod - y took some - bod - y by the hand,____

May - be ev - 'ry - one____ could learn to love____ and un - der - stand.____

Oh - whoah,____ We can real - ly make it bet - ter, yeah.____

(2nd time to Refrain)

Oh - whoah,____ la, la, la, On - ly if we try.____ (We got to)

Student Page 143 *El payo* The accompaniment for this song is found on p. 102.

Student Page 148

Mr. Tambourine Man

Words and Music by Bob Dylan
Arranged by Christopher Hatcher

El payo (The Cowpoke)

English Words by Alice Firgau

Folk Song from Mexico
Arranged by Cameron McGraw

Lazily

1. Es - ta - ba_un pa - yo sen - ta - do_____ en tran - cas de_un co - rral;_____ Y el
1. Oh, Nick, a sad,_ old cow - poke,_ Would sit all day on a fence.____ The

ma - yor - do - mo le di - jo,_____ "No es - tés tris - te, Ni - co - lás."_____ "Si
fore - man saw him and told him,_____ "Your sad - ness does -n't make sense."_____ "Just

quie - res que no_es - té tris - te_____ Lo que pi - da me has de dar."_____ Y el
give me all that I ask for_____ And you'd cheer my low mor - ale."_____ The

ma - yor - do - mo le di - jo,_____ "Ve pi - dien - do, Ni - co - lás."_____
fore - man smiled then and told him,_____ "Well, start ask - ing, Nick, old pal."_____

2. "Necesito treinta pesos,
   Una cuera y un gabán."
   Y el mayordomo le dijo,
   "No hay dinero, Nicolás."
   "Necesito treinta pesos
   Para poderme casar."
   Y el mayordomo le dijo,
   "Ni un real tengo, Nicolás."

2. "I need some thirty *pesos*,
   A jacket, coat, and a hat."
   The foreman smiled then and told him,
   "No money have I for that."
   "I need those thirty *pesos*
   For to marry my sweet gal."
   The foreman smiled then and told him,
   "I have none, my dear, old pal."

Hava nagila

Jewish Folk Song
Arranged by Morton Yanes

Paths of Victory

Words and Music by Bob Dylan
Arranged by Anita P. Davis

Steadily

REFRAIN

Trails of trou-bles,__ Roads of__ bat-tles,__

Paths of vic-to-ry,__ We shall__ walk.

Fine

VERSE

1. The trail is dust-y,__ And my road it might be rough, But the
2. I walked down by the riv-er,__ I turned my__ head up high, I__

104

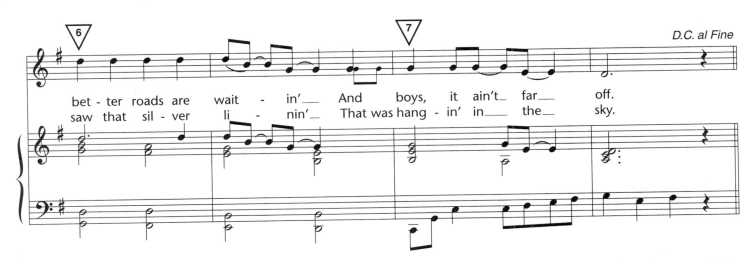

3. The gravel road is bumpy,
It's a hard road to ride,
But there's a clearer road a-waitin'
With the cinders on the side.
Refrain

4. That evening train was rollin',
The hummin' of its wheels,
My eyes they saw a better day
As I looked across the fields.
Refrain

Student Page 158

Scattin' A-Round

Traditional Round
Arranged by Will Schmid
Piano accompaniment by Buddy Skipper & Don Kalbach

O lê lê O Bahía (O Le O La)

Folk Song from Brazil
Arranged by George Almeida

Lo yisa The accompaniment for this song is found on p. 110.

Four Strong Winds *from* Song to a Seagull

Words and Music by Ian Tyson
Arranged by Robert Evans
Piano accompaniment by Alan Seale

winds that blow lone-ly, Sev-en seas that run high, All those things that don't

change, come what may,_____ But our good times are all gone, And I'm

bound for mov-in' on, I'll look for you if I'm ev-er back this way._____

Lo yisa (Vine and Fig Tree)

Hebrew Words from the Book of Isaiah
English Version by Leah Jaffa and Fran Minkoff

Music by Shalom Altman
Arranged by David ben Avraham

Así es mi tierra *(This Is My Land)*

Words and Music by Ignacío Fernandez Esperón
Arranged by Bob Diaz

¡Ay, tie - rra mí - a co-mo es gra - to tu ca - lor!
Oh, my dear coun - try, Wel-come are your gifts of love.

2nd time to next stanza

Sus al - bo - ra - das tan lle - ni - tas, de a - le -
When morn - ing light comes, Peo-ple greet the day with

grí - a. Sus se - re - na - tas tan pro - pi - ci as al a -
glad - ness. In hap - py sing - ing we hear mel - o - dies of

mor.
love.

A - sí es mi tie - rra, flor de la me - lan - co - lí - a.
This is my coun - try, Leav-ing fills me with such sad-ness;

¡Ay, tie - rra mí - a co-mo es gra - to tu ca - lor!
Oh, my dear coun - try, Wel-come are your gifts of love.

Vive l'amour

Traditional College Song
Arranged by Carol Cleveland

1. Let ev-'ry good fel-low now join in a song,
2. Come all you good fel-lows and join join in with me,

Vi - ve la com - pa - gnie!_____ Suc - cess to each oth - er and
And raise up your voic - es in

pass it a - long, Vi - ve la com - pa - gnie!_____
close har - mo - ny,

Vi - ve la, vi - ve la, vi - ve l'a-mour, Vi - ve la, vi - ve la, vi - ve l'a-mour,

Vi - ve l'a-mour, Vi - ve l'a-mour, Vi - ve la com - pa - gnie!_____

Mary Ann

Calypso Song from the West Indies
Arranged by Neil Swanson

Go, My Son

Words and Music by Burson-Nofchissey
Arranged by Linda Williams

Peace Like a River

African American Spiritual
Arranged by Lawrence Eisman

With a strong, steady rhythm

1. I've got peace like a riv - er, I've got peace like a riv - er, I've got

peace like a riv - er in my soul._____ (in my soul.) I've got peace like a

riv-er, I've got peace like a riv-er, I've got peace like a

riv-er in my soul._____ (in my soul.)

1.,2.

3.

soul._____ (in my soul.)

2. I've got joy like a fountain, . . .

3. I've got love like the ocean, . . .

crescendo

f

Let Us Sing Together

Traditional
Arranged by Leslie Jefferson

gain and a-gain. Let us sing a - gain and a-gain, Let us sing a -

gain and a - gain, One and all a de - light - ful song.

Student Page 192

Lost My Gold Ring

Singing Game from Jamaica
Arranged by Donald Scafuri

Playfully

Bid-dy, Bid-dy, hold on, lost my gold ring; One go to Kings-ton, come back a-gain.

New Hungarian Folk Song

Words and Music by Béla Bartók

Now a lone bird seeks her mate so mourn-ful - ly.

High a-bove the corn a lark now earth-ward flies.

Sad her heart, for - lorn a-midst the emp-ty skies. Shel-tered, hid-den

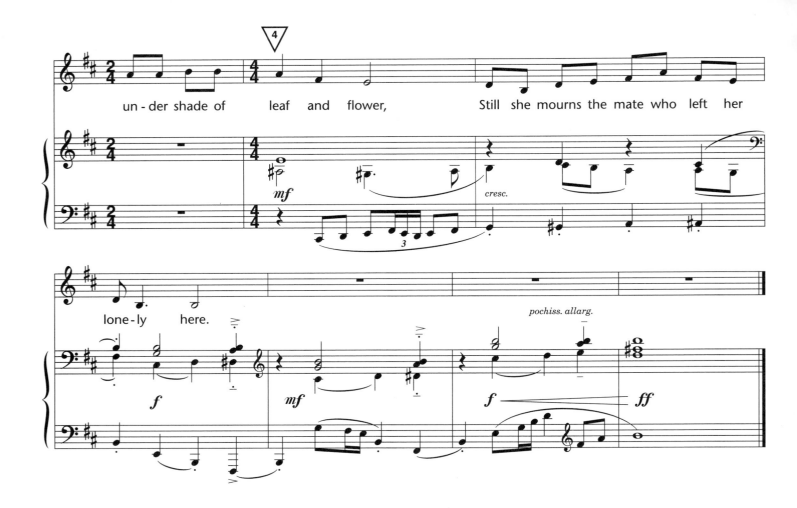

un-der shade of leaf and flower, Still she mourns the mate who left her lone-ly here.

124

Your Friends Shall Be the Tall Wind

Words by Fannie Stearns Davis

Music by Emma Lou Diemer

Smoothly

1. Your friends shall be the tall wind, the riv-er and the tree: The
2. And you shall run and wan-der, and you shall dream and sing of

sun that laughs and march-es, the swal-lows and the sea. Your
brave things___ and bright things be-yond the swal-low's wings. And

prayers shall be the mur-mur of grass-es in the rain; The
you shall en-vy no man, nor hurt your heart with sighs; For

song of wild wood thrush-es that makes God___ glad a-gain.
I will keep you sim-ple, that God may make you wise,

That God may make you wise, that God may make you wise.

125

Like a Bird

Words by E. Bolkovac

Music by Luigi Cherubini
Arranged by Marilyn J. Patterson

Siyahamba

Traditional Freedom Song from South Africa
Arranged by Rick Baitz

ham - ba _____   Si - ya - ham - ba

Si - ya - ham - ba   Si - ya - ham - ba

Kyrie

Round from Suriname
Arranged by Neil Swanson

Solemnly

Ky - ri - e, ky - ri - e e - lei - son.

Ky - ri - e, ky - ri - e e - lei - son.

Ky - ri - e, ky - ri - e___ e - lei - son.

I've Been Everywhere

Words and Music by Geoff Mack
Arranged by Buddy Skipper

Confidently

REFRAIN

I've been ev - 'ry - where, man; I've been ev - 'ry - where, man.

'Cross the des - erts bare, man. I've breathed the moun - tain air, man. Of

trav - el, I've had my share, man. I've been ev - ry - where.

Been to share, man. I

know some place you have-n't been. I've been ev - ry -

where.

1. Reno, Chicago,   Fargo, Minnesota,
2. Boston, Charleston,   Dayton, Louisiana,
3. Louisville, Nashville,   Knoxville, Ombabika,
4. Pittsburgh, Parkersburg,   Gravelburg, Colorado,

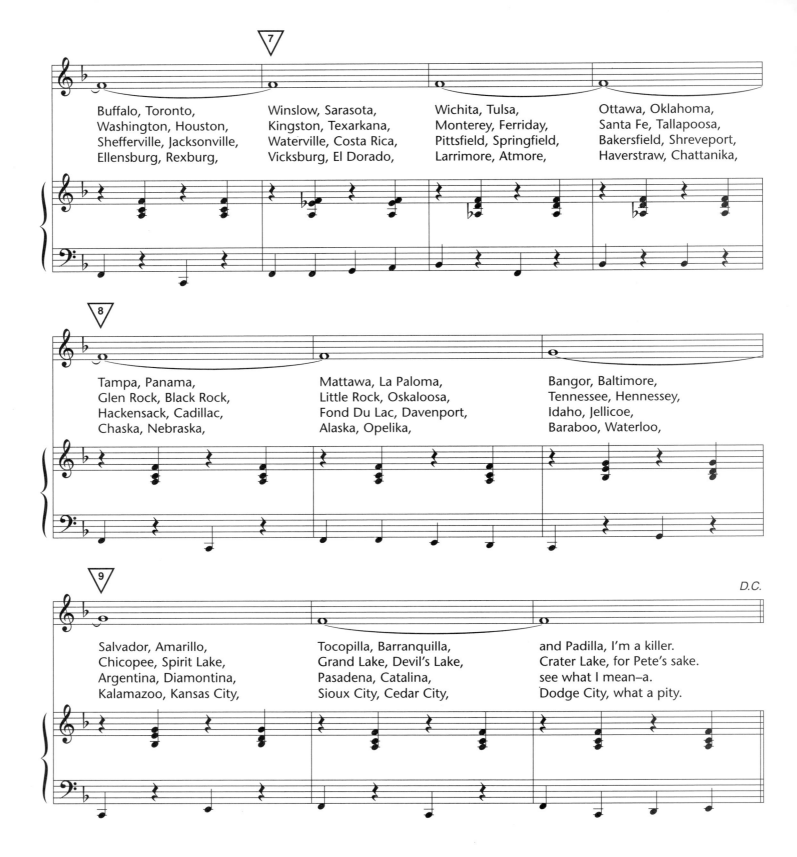

Ise oluwa

Yoruba Folk Song from Nigeria
Arranged by Ting Ho

135

The Water Is Wide

Folk Song from England
Arranged by William Wallace

And we shall cross,_____ my true love and I._____
I care not if_____ I sink or___ swim._____
And fades a - way_____ like morn - ing__ dew._____

This Little Light of Mine

African American Spiritual
Arranged by Linda Twine and Joseph Joubert
Piano Accompaniment by Buddy Skipper

This lit-tle light of mine,_____ I'm gon-na let it shine, Let it shine,__ let it shine,_____ let it shine._____

Gospel feel

let it shine,   let it shine.

Let it shine,   let it shine,   let it shine,   let it shine,

Let it shine,   let it shine,   let it shine.

Sometimes I Feel Like a Motherless Child

African American Spiritual
Arranged by Carol Jay

142

Sun Gonna Shine

Traditional Blues
Arranged by Audrey Schultz

5. You used to be my sugar, but you ain't too sweet no more,
   You used to be my sugar, but you ain't too sweet no more,
   You've got another baby hangin' round your door.

Key to the Highway

Words and Music by Big Bill Broonzy and Charles Segar
Arranged by Carol Jay

Jambalaya (On the Bayou)

Words and Music by Hank Williams
Arranged by Don Kalbach

night I'm gon - na see my *ma cher a - mi-o.*   Pick gui-tar,   fill fruit   jar,   and be

gay-o,   Son of a   gun, we'll have big fun   on the bay-ou.   2. Thi-bo-

Student Page 238

You Are My Sunshine

Words and Music by Jimmie Davis and Charles Mitchell
Arranged by Carol Jay

Tenderly
REFRAIN

You   are   my   sun - shine,_____   my   on - ly   sun - shine;_____   You make me

hap - py_____   when skies are   gray._____   You'll nev - er   know,   dear,_____

146

how much I love you; _____ Please don't take my

Fine **VERSE**

sun - shine a - way. _____ The oth - er night, dear, _____

_ as I lay sleep - ing, _____ I dreamed I held you in my

arms, _____ When I a - woke, dear, _____ I was mis -

D.C. al Fine

tak - en _____ and I hung my head and cried. _____

Green, Green Grass of Home

Words and Music by Curly Putman
Arranged by Billy Joe Lafayette

good   to touch   the   green,   green   grass   of   home.
good   to touch   the   green,   green   grass   of   home.

REFRAIN

Yes, they'll all   come to meet me,   arms__ reach-ing,   smil-ing sweet-ly;   It's

good   to touch the green, green grass   of   home._____

Summertime

Words by Dubose Heyward

Music by George Gershwin
Arranged by William Stickles and Donald Scafuri

Lazily

Sum-mer - time_____ and the liv - in' is eas - y._____ Fish are

jump-in',_____ And the cot - ton is high._____ Oh, your

dad - dy's rich_____ and your ma is good - look - in',_____ So

hush, lit - tle ba - by, don't_ you cry._____ One of these

Don't Be Cruel

Words and Music by Otis Blackwell and Elvis Presley
Arranged by John Girt

Downtown

Words and Music by Tony Hatch
Arranged by Marilyn J. Patterson

ne - on signs are pret - ty. How can you lose?___ The lights___ are much
fore the night is o - ver, hap - py a - gain.___

bright - er___ there,_ you can for - get all your trou - bles for - get all your cares.__ So go

Down - town. Things-'ll be great_ when you're Down - town. No fin - er place_ for sure,

D.C. First Time
Fine Second Time

Down - town. Ev - 'ry - thing's wait - ing for you.

Surfin' U.S.A.

Words by Brian Wilson

Music by Chuck Berry
Arranged by Buddy Skipper

1. If ev-'ry-bod-y had an
2. We'll all be plan-nin' out a

o - cean_____ a - cross the U. S. A.,_____
route_____ we're gon - na take real soon._____

Then ev-'ry-bod-y'd be surf - in'_____ like Cal-i-for-ni - a._____
We're wax-in' down_ our surf - boards,_ we can't_ wait for June._

All o - ver Man - hat - tan,___ and down Do - he - ny way.___
All o - ver La Jol - la,___ at Wai - a - me - a Bay.___

Ev - 'ry - bod - y's gone surf - in',___
Ev - 'ry - bod - y's gone surf - in',___

Surf - in' U. S. A.___
Surf - in' U. S. A.___

Riendo el río corre (Run, Run, River)

English Words by Sue Ellen LaBelle

Words and Music by Tish Hinojosa
Arranged by David Eddleman

de   tu   em - pe - sar,_____
pien - sas   al - can - zar,_____
where   your jour - ney be - gan,_____
gone   to   reach_____ the_____ sea,_____

5

Cuén - ta - me_____ de_____ pie - dra y pe - na_____ que
Co - mo sue - ño_____ de_____ la lu - na_____ que
Tell   a - bout_____ the_____ pla - ces_____ you
Whis - p'rings of_____ your_____ trav - els_____ seem

6   *D.S. al Coda*

que   lle - vas_____ al_____ mar._____
me   das   para_____ so - ñar._____
passed   a - long_____ the_____ way._____
like   a   dream_____ to_____ me._____

⊕ Coda

en - do el rí - o_____   co - rre._____
laugh - ter runs_____ the_____ riv - er._____

It's Time

Words and Music by Lebo M., John Van Tongeren, and Jay Rifkin
Arranged by Mark A. Miller

(Oh, _____) Let's ce-le-brate.　　　　　(Oh, _____) Let's

ce-le-brate.　　　　　(Oh, _____) Let's ce-le-brate.

D.C.　　　*Fine*

Student Page 274

Nana Kru

Traditional Song from the Kou Tribe of Liberia (Adapted)
Arranged by Mark A. Miller

Flowing

Na-na,　Na-na Kru,　　Na-na,　Na-na, Na-na

Kru,　Jump in-to my ca-noe,　Na-na,　you know that I love you.

Take Time in Life

Folk Song from Liberia
Arranged by Audrey Schultz

Banuwa

Folk Song from Liberia
Arranged by George Winston

Everybody Loves Saturday Night

Folk Song from West Africa
Arranged by Audrey Schultz

Water Come a Me Eye

Folk Song from Trinidad
Arranged by Mark A. Miller

Má Teodora

Folk Song from Cuba
Arranged by Mary Jean Nelson

Asadoya

English Words by D. G. Britton

Folk Song from Okinawa
Arranged by Bruce Saylor

Alumot *(Sheaves of Grain)*

English Words by Sue Ellen LaBelle

Harvest Song from Israel
Arranged by Vlad Rosco

Steadfastly

Ye - la - dim_____ na - gi - la ve - na - sov bim - cho - lot!
Har - vest time has__ come! We'll cir - cle round and dance. Let's re - joice!

Shi - bo - lim_____ hiv - shi - lu. Ne' e - sof a - lu - mot!
Sheaves of wheat are__ ripe, we'll sing a song of joy. Raise your voice!

A - lu - mot shel za - hav ha - sa - deh ra - chav, ra - chav.
Gold - en sheaves, grain and leaves, we will be the gath - er - ers,

Ba - sa - deh u - va - nir, shi - ru ze - mer la - ka - tsir!
In the field, land's great yield, Let's sing to the har - vest - ers!

172

Al yadee

Words Adapted by Sally Monsour

Ancient Arabic Chant
Arranged by Chris Hatcher

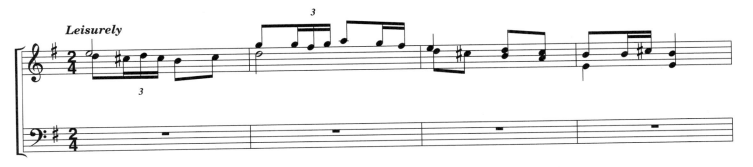

1. *Al* ya - dee, ya - dee, ya - dee; Come and take a walk with me;
2. *Al* ya - dee, ya - dee, ya - dee; Come and take a walk with me;

In the mead - ow we shall see; Birds are fly - ing, fly - ing free.
To the val - ley, near the sea; We will al - ways hap - py be.

Al ya - dee, ya - dee, ya - dee;____ Come and take a walk with__ me.
Al ya - dee, ya - dee, ya - dee;____ Come and take a walk with__ me.

By the Waters of Babylon

Words from Psalm 137

Caribbean Folk Song
Arranged by Don Kalbach

Quietly *(Add harmony part on D.C. only)*

By the wa-ters of Bab - y-lon, Where we sat down, And there we

wept When we re-mem-bered Zi - on. But the wick - ed

car-ry us a-way cap-tiv - i - ty, Re - quire of us a song.

How can you sing the Lord's own song in a strange land?

Fine

D.C. al Fine

175

On My Way *from* Violet

Words by Brian Crawley

Music by Jeanine Tesori
Vocal Arrangement by Michael Rafter
Arranged by Betsy Washington

Bright anthem

Be - fore an - oth - er sun - rise___ wakes me, Be - fore an - oth - er night is___ gone, I'll find out where this high - way___ takes me,___ You know I've got to trav - el___

Left my trou-bles all be - hind me. Back there when I climbed on

board. Jor - dan Riv - er's where you'll_ find me. It's

wide but not too wide to ford. And as I'm go - in' a -

long, I car - ry with me prom - is - es that can't go wrong,

As I trav-el on._____ As I trav-el on_____

my way._____

Run! Run! Hide!

Words and Music by Linda Twine
Adapted from the Cantata *"Changed My Name"*

Tubman: *There was one of two things I had a
right to, liberty or death; if I could not
have one, I would have the other;
for no man should take me alive.*

The Rhythm Is Gonna Get You

Words and Music by Gloria Estefan and Enrique Garcia
Arranged by Buddy Skipper

the rhy-thm is gon-na get__ you.
it, the rhy-thm is gon-na get__ you.

At night_ throw the cov - ers on your head,_
No clue_ of what's hap - pen - ing to you._

You pre - tend like you were dead,_
But be - fore this night is through,_

One Moment In Time

Words and Music by Albert Hammond and John Bettis
Arranged by Buddy Skipper

be,   when all____ of my dreams__ are a heart - beat a - way____ and the

an - swers__ are all   up__ to me.   Give__ me__

one   mo - ment__ in time,   when I'm

rac - ing__ with des - ti - ny.__

Then, in that_ one mo - ment_ in_ time___ I will

be, I will be,_ I will be free._____

Mama Don't 'Low

Folk Song from the United States
Arranged by Don Kalbach

1. Ma - ma don't 'low no gui - tar play - in' 'round here,
2. Ma - ma don't 'low no ban - jo pick - in' 'round here,

Ma - ma don't 'low no gui - tar play - in' 'round here,
Ma - ma don't 'low no ban - jo pick - in' 'round here,

I don't care what Ma - ma don't 'low, Gon - na play my gui - tar an - y - how,
I don't care what Ma - ma don't 'low, Gon - na pick my ban - jo an - y - how,

Ma - ma don't 'low no gui - tar play - in' 'round here.
Ma - ma don't 'low no ban - jo pick - in' 'round here.

Corta la caña   (Head for the Canefields)

English Words by Aura Kontra

Folk Song from Puerto Rico
Arranged by Audre Morrison

- cha na die quie - re tra - ba - jar.
- ed no one wants to come a - long.

Cor - ta la ca - ña, ca - ñe - ro, cór - ta - la._____
Head for the cane - fields each morn - ing, cut them down._

Cor - ta la ca - ña, ca - ñe - ro, cór - ta - la._____
Head for the cane - fields till sun - set, cut them down._

Boil Them Cabbage Down

Pioneer Song from the United States
Arranged by Neil Swanson

Worried Man Blues

Traditional Blues
Arranged by Ting Ho

Skye Boat Song

Words by Sir Harold Boulton

Music by Annie MacLeod
Arranged by James Rooker

Tom Dooley

Folk Song from the United States
Arrangement by Cheryl Terhune Cronk

Down in the Valley

Folk Song from Kentucky
Arranged by Neil Swanson

Cuando pa' Chile me voy (Leavin' for Chile)

English Words by Aura Kontra

Cueca from Chile
Arranged by Joyce Kalbach

cue - ca y la zam - ba,
cue - ca and zam - ba.
Dos pun - tas tie - ne_el ca - mi - no y_en las dos

al - guien me_a - guar - da.
some - one a - waits me.
al - guien me_a - guar - da.
some - one a - waits me.

2. *En Chile bailo la cueca,*
En Cuyo bailo la zamba, } 2 times
En Chile con las chilenas,
Con las otras en Calingasta. } 2 times
Vida trist, vida alegre,
Es la vida del arriero, } 2 times
Penitas en el camino,
Y risas al fin del sendero. } 2 times
Refrain.

2. I dance the *cueca* in Chile,
In Cuyo I do the *zamba,* } 2 times
Dancing with the girls from Chile,
Or with the ones from Calingasta. } 2 times
Days can be happy or sad,
The life of an *arriero.* } 2 times
Troubles face me on my journey,
But laughter awaits me at nightfall. } 2 times
Refrain.

Ezekiel Saw the Wheel

African American Spiritual
Arranged by Larry Eisman

grace of God, It's a wheel in a wheel, 'Way in the mid-dle of the

air.

Fine **VERSE**

1. Some go to church for to sing and shout,
2. One of these days 'bout twelve o'-clock,

'Way in the mid-dle of the air, Be - fore six months they're
'Way in the mid-dle of the air, This old world gonna

D.S. al Fine

shout - ed out! 'Way in the mid - dle of the air. E -
reel and rock! 'Way in the mid - dle of the air. E -

209

Just a Snap-Happy Blues

Words and Music by Norma Jean Luckey
Arranged by John Girt

doo bah doo bah___ dee doo bah doo bah doo wah___

Dah bah doo bah___ bah___ bah dah Dah bah doo bah___ bah___

dop Dah bah doo bah___ bah___ bah dah,

Dah bah doo bah___ bah___ dop, wah wah

wah da, Dah bah dah bah dop bah dah___ *Fine*

(⌢ Last time only!)

Doo wee doo bop

Doo bah doo bah doo wah,___

Dee doo bah doo bop doo wah doo bop

dop, Doo bah doo bah— bah— bah dah

Doo bah doo bah doo wah,—

Dee doo bah doo bop Doo wee

Dah bah doo bah— bah— dop Wah wah

Student Page 383

A Gift to Share

Words and Music by Rollo A. Dilworth
Arranged by Buddy Skipper

216

gift to be free. I must share it_____ ev - er - y day in hope

that the gifts of the ones a - round me will come my way.

I'll shout it high, I'll shout it low that I must share this

I'll shout it. Yes, I'll shout that I must share this

that the gifts of the ones a-round me will come my way.

gifts of the ones a-round me will come my way.

I'm a gift. I'm a gift. I'm

I'm a gift. I'm a gift. I'm

a gift. I'm a gift.

a gift. I'm a gift.

The Gospel Train

African American Spiritual
Arranged by Shirley W. McRae
Piano accompaniment by Mark A. Miller

1 All a - board!____ All a -

2 sister, don't be vain,____ But come and get your tick - et, Be read - y for the

3 sister, don't be vain,____ Get your tick - et, read - y for the

Ⓐ

1 board! Lit - tle chil-dren, lit - tle chil-dren,

2 train. Get on board, lit - tle chil-dren, get on board, lit - tle chil-dren, get on

3 train. Lit - tle chil-dren, lit - tle chil-dren,

Fais do do *(Go to Sleep)*

English Words by Sue Ellen LaBelle

Acadian Folk Song
Arranged by Susan Brumfield

Fais do do, 'co-las, mon p'tit frè - re,
Go to sleep, my dear lit-tle broth - er,

227

233

Shalom aleichem

Traditional Jewish Song
Arranged by Allan E. Naplan
Adapted by Donald Kalbach

Cantaré, cantarás   (I Will Sing, You Will Sing)

English Words by Eileen Mahood-José

Words and Music by Albert Hammond and Juan Carlos Calderón
Arranged by Richard Kaller
Piano accompaniment by Buddy Skipper

239

7

del sen-de-ro.
da-mos la ma-no
_ us to-geth-er._
_ of your dream,_

Bri - lla - rá
Siem - pre ha - brá
And our hopes
We'll make sure

8

co-mo un sol
un lu-gar
and our prayers,
there's a place

Que i-lu - mi - na el mun - ser -
Pa - ra to - do ser
We will make them last
For ev - 'ry hu -

1.

do en - te - ro.
hu - ma
for - ev - er
man be

2.

(Last time repeat refrain ad lib.)

no.
ing.

Rit.- - - - - - - - - - - - - - - - - - - -

Vem kan segla? *(Who Can Sail?)*

English Words by Gunilla Marcus-Luboff

Folk Song from Finland
Arranged by Carl-Bertil Agnestig

2. Jag kan segla forütan vind,
jag kan ro utan åror,
men ej skiljas från vänen min
utan att fälla tårar.

2. I can sail when the winds won't blow,
need no oars for my rowing.
I can't part with my heart aglow,
part when your tears are flowing.

Ding Dong! Merrily on High

Arranged by Howard Cable
Edited by Henry Leck

Ding dong! Mer-ri - ly on high, _____ the

Ding dong! Mer-ri - ly on high, _____ the

baby born of Mary. Glo_____ glo_____

_____ Glo_____ gloria, hosanna in ex-

glo_____ gloria, hosanna in ex-

celsis!_____

celsis!_____

sound the stee - ple bell for joy - ous news___ we are

bell_____ for joy - ous news we are

bring - ing. Glo - - - - - - - - -

bring - ing. Ding dong ding dong,

Goin' to Boston

Folk Song from the United States
Arranged by Shirley W. McRae
Accompaniment adapted by Don Kalbach

Won't we look pur-ty in the ball-room, won't we look pur-ty in the ball-room,

won't we look pur-ty in the ball-room, ear-lye in the morn-in'.

swing your part-ner all the way to Bos-ton, ear-lye in the morn-in'.

Won't we look pur-ty in the ball-room, won't we look pur-ty in the

Won't we look pur-ty in the ball-room, won't we look pur-ty in the

ball-room, won't we look pur-ty in the ball-room, ear-lye in the morn-in'.

ball-room, won't we look pur-ty in the ball-room, ear-lye in the morn-in'.

5. Get out the way, you'll get run o - ver, get out the way, you'll get run o - ver,

get out the way, you'll get run o - ver, ear - lye in the morn - in'.

(Clap)

Won't we look pur - ty in the ball - room, won't we look pur - ty in the ball - room,

won't we look pur - ty in the ball - room, ear - lye in the morn - in'.

Won't we look pur - ty in the ball - room, won't we look pur - ty in the ball - room,

won't we look pur - ty in the ball - room, ear - lye in the morn-in'!

Under the Same Sun

Words and Music by Clifford Carter
Arranged By Buddy Skipper

Ev'-ry-bod-y has a song in___ their heart, though some - times___ it's hard to sing.___ So man-y voic-es go un - heard,___ it's time to___ start___ lis - ten - ing.___ Oh,_____ oh._____

Oh,_____ oh._____ oh._____ Though we

The United Nations

Words by Harold Rome

Music by Dmitri Shostakovich
Arranged by John Detroy

1. The sun and the stars all are ring - ing,_____ With song ris - ing
2. Take heart all you na - tions swept un - der,_____ With pow - ers of
3. As sure as the sun meets the morn - ing,_____ And riv - ers go

from the____ earth._____ The hope of hu - man - i - ty
dark - ness that ride,_____ The wrath of the peo - ple shall
down to the sea,_____ A new day for all is____

sing - ing,_____ A hymn to a new world in birth.
thun - der,_____ Re - lent - less as time and the tide.
dawn - ing,_____ Our chil - dren shall live proud and free!

U - ni - ted Na - tions on the march with flags un - furl'd,_____ To-

geth - er fight for vic - to - ry, a free New World._____ To - ___

One People

English Words by Noreen Tourangeau and Debbie Nicotine

Music and Cree Words by Josef Naytowhow
Arranged by Buddy Skipper

We are all ___ one peo - ple, We all come from one cre - a - tion ___ 'way on high. ___ We are all ___ one ___ na - tion ___ un - der one ___ great sky, ___ you and I. ___

We are all _____ one_ peo-ple, ____ We are all _____ one_ co-lor____ in his eye._

Kah - kiyaw kiya - naw pēy - ak ayi - si - ni-wak. Kah-kiyaw ki -

toh - ci - naw kih - ci ma - ni - tow.___   *Kah - kiyaw kiya -*

naw oh - ci pēy - ak as - kiy sī - pi pēy - ak kī - sik ki - ya - naw.___

Kah - kiyaw kiya - naw pēy - ak ayi - si - ni - wak. Kih - ci ma -

ni - tow peya - kwan kis - nak - si - na - naw o - ski - si - kwa.___

I Am But a Small Voice

Original Words by Odina E. Batnag

English Words and Music by Roger Whittaker
Arranged by Ian Williams

Come, young cit-i-zens of the world; We are one, we are one.

one. _____ We have one hope, we have one dream, and

with one voice we sing.

small_ dream:_   To   smile up-on the sun,   Be   free to dance_ and sing,   Be

D.S. al Fine

free to sing_ my song   to ev - 'ry - one.

Student Page 434

The Purple People Eater

Words and Music by Sheb Wooley
Arranged by Mark A. Miller

Outlandishly

VERSE

1. Well, I   saw   the   thing_   a - com - in'
2. Well, he   came down to   earth_   and he___

One - eyed,   one - horned,   fly - in' pur - ple peo - ple eat - er,   One - eyed,   one - horned,
Pigeon - toed,   under - growed,   fly - in' pur - ple peo - ple eat - er,   He   wears   short   shorts,

fly - in'   pur - ple   peo - ple   eat - er,   Sure   looked   strange   to   me.___
friend - ly   lit - tle   peo - ple   eat - er,

1.

2.

What   a   sight   to   see.___

Loigratong

English Words by Alice Firgau

Folk Song from Thailand
Arranged by Ting Ho

With good cheer

1

wan pen___ deup sip song___ nam gau
The ri - ver is ris - ing, the

2

nong tem ta - ling rao tang lai___ chai ying sa - nook gan -
moon, it is full. Ev - 'ry - one feels so hap - py and

3

jing wan loi - gra-tong loi loi - gra-tong loi loi - gra-tong loi - gra-
glad on Loi - gra-tong. Loi, Loi - gra-tong, Loi, Loi - gra-tong, Loi - gra-

4

tong gan lah-ow koh___ churn nong kay oh ock ma lum wong lum
tong. Come, float your boat, then join the dance with me. We

273

S'vivon (Dreydl)

Hebrew Words by L. Kipnis
English Words by Sue Ellen LaBelle and David Eddleman

Folk Song from Israel
Arranged by Donald Kalbach

Winter Song

Words and Music by Stephen Paulus
Arranged by Mark A. Miller

ring,   ring, ching   ring.

5 VERSE
mp

1. Win - ter songs are   for   ev - 'ry - one,   Young,   old,
2. Long   nights   and   cold win - try   winds,   Snow,   snow,

6
mf

peo - ple so   wear - y,   Young,   old,   peo - ple so   cheer-y who
i - ci - cles long,   warm   to   win - ter's song   so

(2nd time to next strain) **8** *ff countermelody*

Sing,   sing a win - ter song,

7
cresc.   *ff melody*

Sing,   sing,   sing,   sing.   Bells_ are ring - ing, they're ring-ing for you and me,
Sing,   sing,   sing,   sing,   sing.

Sing, sing a hap-py song,___ Ring, ring, ring, ring,

Play-ing a light and a won-der-ful mel-o-dy, Ring, ring, ring, ring,

rit. mf

Ring, ring, ring, ring. Ring, ring, ring, ring. Ring!___

Ring, ring, ring, ring. Ring, ring, ring, ring. Ring!___

Student Page 444

Caroling, Caroling

Words by Wihla Hutson

Music by Alfred Burt
Arranged by Mark A. Miller

Joyously

1. Car - ol - ing, car - ol - ing, now we go; Christ - mas bells are ring - ing!
2. Car - ol - ing, car - ol - ing, thru the town; Christ - mas bells are ring - ing!

Gloria, Gloria

Music by Franz Joseph Haydn

Good King Wenceslas

Traditional
Arranged by Wayne Roe

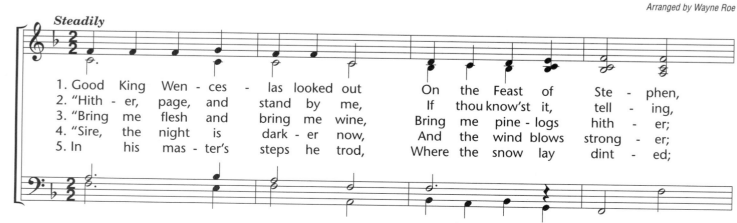

2

When the snow lay round a - bout, Deep and crisp and e - ven;
Yon - der peas - ant, who is he? Where and what his dwell - ing?"
Thou and I will see him dine, When we bear them thi - ther."
Fails my heart, I know not how, I can go no long - er."
Heat was in the ver - y sod Which the saint had print - ed.

3

Bright - ly shone the moon that night, Though the frost was cru - el,
"Sire, he lives a good league hence, Un - der - neath the moun - tain;
Page and mon - arch forth they went, Forth they went to - geth - er;
"Mark my foot - steps, good my page! Tread thou in them bold - ly;
There - fore, Chris - tian folk, be sure, Wealth or rank pos - sess - ing;

4

When a poor man came in sight, Gath - 'ring win - ter fu - el.
Right a - gainst the for - est fence, By Saint Ag - nes' foun - tain."
Through the rude wind's wild la - ment, And the bit - ter wea - ther.
Thou shalt find the win - ter's rage Freeze they blood less cold - ly."
Ye who now will bless the poor, Shall your-selves find bless - ing.

The Joy of Kwanzaa

Words and Music by Reggie Royal
Piano Accompaniment Adapted by Don Kalbach

Sincerely

There are times_____ of cel-e-bra - tion_____ in our lives, here or

far a - way,_____ That our love_____ binds us to-geth - er,_____ and this

com - mon bond re - mains. See the lights,_____ they shine so bright -
_____ in the kin-a -

This is the joy of Kwan - zaa. Cel - e - bra - ting com - mu - ni - ty,_____

2nd time to Coda

This is the joy of Kwan - zaa.

D.S. Coda

Can - dles burn   And the road of life be - fore_ us   is a

mu - ni - ty,_____ This is the joy of Kwan - zaa,

This is the joy of Kwan - zaa._____

Abraham, Martin, and John

Words and Music by Dick Holler
Vocal Arrangement by Joan R. Hillsman
Arranged by Joseph Joubert

seems the good die young,— But I just looked a - round and he's
o - ver the hill—— with—— A - bra - ham, Mar - tin, and

1.,2.,3.

4.

Fine

1.,2. gone.——————————— Has

3. gone.——————————— John.——————

(To Refrain)

REFRAIN

Did-n't you love—— the things they—— stood for?

Did-n't they try____ to find some good for you and me? And we'll be free,

Some - day soon, it's gonna be____one day. Has

D.S. al Fine

Free at Last

African American Spiritual
Vocal Arrangement by Joan R. Hillsman
Arranged by Joseph Joubert

I Wish I Knew How It Would Feel to Be Free

Words by Billy Taylor and Dick Dallas

Music by Billy Taylor
Arranged by Buryl Red
Piano Accompaniment by Mark A. Miller

1. I wish I knew how____ it would feel____ to be free.____ I
2. I wish I could share____ all the love____ in my heart,____ Re -
3. I wish I could give____ all I'm long - ing to give.____ I
4. I wish I could be____ like a bird____ in the sky;____ How

wish I could break____ all these chains____ hold-ing me.____ I
move all the bars____ that still keep____ us a - part.____ I
wish I could live____ like I'm long - ing to live.____ I
sweet it would be____ if I found____ I could fly.____ I'd

294

wish   I   could say____   all the things____   I should say,____   Say 'em loud,_
wish   you could know____   what it means____   to   be   me;____   Then you'd see__
wish   I   could do____   all the things____   I   can   do;____   Though I'm 'way_
soar   to   the sun____   and look down____   at   the sea;____   Then I'd sing,_

_   say 'em clear,____   for   the whole____   world to   hear.____
_   and a - gree,____   ev - 'ry man____   should be free.____
_   o - ver - due,____   I'd be start - ing a - new.____
_   'cause I'd know____   how   it feels____   to   be free.____

Eres tú *(Touch the Wind)*

English words by Mike Hawker

Words and Muisc by Juan Carlos Calderón

Love in Any Language

Words and Music by Jon Mohr and John Mays
Arranged by John Higgins

though our words are all__ u - nique,_ our hearts are still the same._____

REFRAIN

Love in an - y lan - guage,_ straight from the heart,_

Pulls us all_ to-geth - er,_ nev - er a - part._ And once we learn_ to speak_ it,_

all the world__ will hear,__ Love in an - y lan - guage__ flu-ent-ly spo - ken__ here. We teach the young__ our dif-f'renc-es, yet look how we're the same.__ We love to laugh,__ to dream our__ dreams,

2nd time to Coda

we know the sting of pain. From Len - in - grad____ to Lex-ing-ton, the

farm - er loves____ his land.____ And fa - thers all____ get mist - y - eyed____ to

give their daugh-ter's hand._____ Oh____ may-be when we re-al-ize____ how

much there is____ to share,__ We'll find too much in com - mon__ to pre-

tend it is-n't there._____ flu-ent-ly spo - ken__ here. Though the

rhet - o - ric__ of gov - ern-ments may keep us worlds__ a - part,__

304

Las mañanitas

English Words by Lupe Allegria

Folk Song from Mexico
Arranged by James Roberts

Flowing

1
Es - tas son   las ma - ña -
Hear us   sing   las ma - ña -

2
ni - tas Que can - ta - ba el Rey Da - vid,   A las mu - cha-chas bo -
ni - tas as the morn - ing light ap - pears,   And the gen - tle bird will

3
ni - tas Se las can - ta - mos a - quí.   Des - pier - ta, mi bien, des -
join   in the hap-py mu - sic he   hears.   Oh,   wake   up and see the

America

Words by Samuel Francis Smith

Traditional Melody

3. Let music swell the breeze,
And ring from all the trees
Sweet freedom's song;
Let mortal tongues awake,
Let all that breathe partake,
Let rocks their silence break,
The sound prolong.

4. Our fathers' God, to Thee,
Author of liberty,
To Thee we sing;
Long may our land be bright
With Freedom's holy light,
Protect us by Thy might,
Great God, our King!

America, the Beautiful

Words by Katharine Lee Bates

Music by Samuel A. Ward

Majestically

1. O beau - ti - ful for spa - cious skies, For am - ber waves of grain, For
2. O beau - ti - ful for pil - grim feet, Whose stern im - pas - sioned stress A
3. O beau - ti - ful for pa - triot dream That sees be - yond the years Thine

pur - ple moun - tain maj - es - ties A - bove the fruit - ed plain! A -
thor - ough - fare for free - dom beat A - cross the wil - der - ness! A -
al - a - bas - ter cit - ies gleam, Un - dimmed by hu - man tears! A -

mer - i - ca! A - mer - i - ca! God shed His grace on thee And
mer - i - ca! A - mer - i - ca! God mend thine ev - 'ry flaw, Con -
mer - i - ca! A - mer - i - ca! God shed his grace on thee And

crown thy good with broth - er - hood From sea to shin - ing sea!
firm thy soul in self - con - trol, Thy lib - er - ty in law!
crown they good with broth - er - hood From sea to shin - ing sea!

The Star-Spangled Banner

Words by Francis Scott Key

Music by John Stafford Smith

CREDITS AND ACKNOWLEDGMENTS

Cover Photography: Jade Albert for Scott Foresman.

Cover Design: Steven Curtis Design, Inc.

Electronic Production: Martini Graphic Services.

Acknowledgments

3: "Your Life Is Now" by John Melloncamp, George M.Green, Little B. Publishing, EMI. April Music Inc. 5: "A Brand New Day" by Luther Vandross. ©1975 WB Music Corp. (ASCAP). All Rights Reserved Used by Permission. WARNER BROS. PUBLICATIONS U.S. INC., Miami, FL 33014 11: "Lean On Me" words and music by Bill Withers. All Rights Reserved. Used by Permission. WARNER BROS. PUBLICATIONS U.S. INC. Miami FL 33014 15: "Magnolia" by Tish Hinojosa. © 1996 WB Music Corp. (ASCAP) & Manazo Music (ASCAP). All Rights administered by WB Music Corp. All Rights Reserved. Used by Permission. WARNER BROS. PUBLICATIONS U.S. INC., Miami, FL 33014 17: "Gonna Build a Mountain" From the Musical Production *Stop the World - I Want to Get Off* Words and music by Leslie Bricusse and Anthony Newley. © Copyright 1961 (Renewed) TRO Essex Music Ltd., London, England. TRO - Ludlow Music, Inc., New York, New York, controls all publication rights for the U.S.A. and Canada. Used by Permission. 18: "Put on a Happy Face" from *Bye Bye Birdie* words by Lee Adams; music by Charles Strouse. All Rights Reserved. Used by Permission. WARNER BROS. PUBLICATIONS U.S. INC., Miami, FL. 33014 26: "Wai Bamba" a Shona Wedding Song from *Let Your Voice Be Heard! : songs from Ghana and Zimbabwe* by Abraham Kobina Adzenya, Dumisani Maraire and Judith Cook Tucker. 28: "Rock and Roll Is Here To Stay" words and music by David White. © 1957 by Singular Publishing Co. Copyright Renewed by Arc Music Corporation. All Rights Reserved. Used by Permission. International Copyright Secured. 30: "Give My Regards to Broadway," Music by George M. Cohan. Arranged by Lynn Freeman Olson from *Piano for Pleasure*, 3rd Edition by Martha Hilley & Lynn Freeman Olson. Copyright (c) 1998 by Wadsworth Publishing Company. Reprinted with permission of Wadsworth, an imprint of the Wadsworth Group, a division of Thomson Learning, Fax 800-730-2215. 32: "Farewell to Tarwathie" (Adieu to My Comrades) Folk Song from Scotland from *The Singing Islands* by Peggy Seeger and Ewan McColl. All Rights Reserved. Used by Permission. WARNER BROS. PUBLICATIONS U.S. INC., Miami, FL 33014. 34: "My Dear Companion" by Jean Ritchie. © 1976 Jean Ritchie, Geordie Music Publishing Co. Reprinted with permission. 36: "El Condor Pasa" from *THE MELODY BOOK* by Patricia Hackett Englewood Cliffs, NJ © 1983, Prentice-Hall, Inc. 43: "What A Wonderful World" by George David Weiss and Bob Thiele. © 1967 Range Road Music Inc. and Quartet Music Inc. © Renewed 1995 George David Weiss and Bob Thiele. Right for George David Weiss assigned to Abilene Music, Inc. All Rights Reserved. Used by Permission. WARNER BROS. PUBLICATIONS U.S. INC., Miami, FL. 33014 46: "Sing a Song of Peace" by Jill Gallina. Copyright © 1991 by Shawnee Press, Inc. (ASCAP). International Copyright Secured. All Rights Reserved. Reprinted by Permission. 48: "Don't Cry for Me, Argentina" music by Andrew Lloyd Webber, words by Tim Rice. ©1976, 1977 Evita Music Ltd. All Rights for U.S. and Canada controlled and administered by Universal-MCA Music Publishing, a division of Universal Studios, In. All Rights Reserved. Used by permission. WARNER BROS. PUBLICATIONS U.S. INC., Miami FL 33014 54: "Do, Re, Mi, Fa" from *150 Rounds and Canons*. 58: "Blue Skies" by Irving Berlin. © 1927 by Irving Berlin: renewed. 60: "Bridges" written by Bill Staines. Copyright © 1983 Mineral River Music (BMI). Administered by Bug Music. All Rights Reserved. Used by Permission. 61: "Birthday" by John Lennon and Paul McCartney, © 1968 Northern Songs Limited. 64: "I Got Rhythm" words by Ira Gershwin music by George Gershwin. All Rights Reserved, Used by Permission. WARNER BROS. PUBLICATIONS U.S. INC., Miami, FL 33014 66: "Music Goes With Anything" by Sarah and Robert Sterling. Copyright © 1981 by Shawnee Press, Inc. (ASCAP). International Copyright Secured. All Rights Reserved. Reprinted by Permission. 72: "Hit Me with a Hot Note and Watch Me Bounce," by Duke Ellington and Don George. © 1945 (Renewed). EMI Robbins Catalog Inc. All Rights Reserved. Used by Permission. WARNER BROS. PUBLICATIONS U.S. INC. Miami FL 33014 74: "At The Same Time" by Ann Hampton Callaway. © 1997 WB Music Corp. (ASCAP), Halaron Music (ASCAP), Emmanuel Music Corp. (ASCAP) & Works Of Heart Publishing (ASCAP). All rights administered by WB Music Corp. All Rights Reserved. Used by Permission. WARNER BROS. PUBLICATIONS U.S. INC., Miami, FL 33014 80: "Swanee" by Irving Caesar and George Gershwin. © 1919 (Renewed) WB Music Corp. & Irving Caesar Music Corp. All Rights administered by WB Music Corp. All Rights Reserved. Used by Permission. WARNER BROS. PUBLICATIONS U.S. INC., Miami, FL. 33014 83: "Dance for the Nations" words and music by John (J) Krumm.

Used with permission of the author. 84: "Catch A Falling Star" by Paul Vance and Lee Pockriss. Copyright © by Music Sales Corporation and Emily Music Corporation. International Copyright Secured. All Rights Reserved. Reprinted by Permission. 88: "Strike Up the Band" words and music by George Gershwin.All Rights Reserved. Used by Permission. WARNER BROS. PUBLICATIONS U.S. INC., Miami, FL 33014 95: "Give a Little Love" words and music by Al Hammond & Diane Warren. All Rights Reserved. Used by Permission. WARNER BROS. PUBLICATIONS INC., Miami, FL 33014. 100: "Mr. Tambourine Man," Words and music by Bob Dylan. Copyright © 1964, 1965 by Warner Bros. Inc. Copyright © renewed 1992, 1993 by Special Rider Music. International Copyright Secured. All Rights Reserved. Reprinted by permission of Music Sales Corporation (ASCAP) 104: "Paths of Victory" words and music by Bob Dylan. Copyright Renewed 1992 by Special Rider Music. International Copyright Secured. All Rights Reserved. Reprinted by permission of Music Sales Corporation (ASCAP). 108: "Four Strong Winds" from *Song to a Seagull*. Words and music by Ian Tyson. All rights reserved. Used by permission. WARNER BROS. PUBLICATIONS U.S. INC., Miami, FL 33014. 110: "Vine and Fig Tree" adapted by Leah Jaffa, music by Shalom Altman. 111: "Así es mi tierra" by Ignacío Fernandez Esperon. 116: "Go, My Son" by Burson-Nofchissey. 122: "New Hungarian Folk Song" from *Mikrokosmos*, Vol. 5, No. 127 Copyright 1940 by Hawkes and Son (London) Ltd. Reprinted by permission of Boosey and Hawkes, Inc. 125: "Your Friends Shall Be the Tall Wind," Words by Fannie Stearns Davis, Music by Emma Lou Diemer. © 1970, 1973, 1979 Gemini Press. Inc. Reprinted by permission. 126: "Like a Bird" words by E. Bolkovac, music by Luigi Cherubini, from *150 Rounds and Canons*. 132: "I've Been Everywhere" words and music by Geoff Mack. (Rightsong Music Inc.) 135: "Ise Oluwa," Yoruba Folk Song From Nigeria, arranged by Nitanju Bolade Casel. 144: "Key to the Highway" by Charles Segar and Big Bill Broonzy. © 1941, 1971, (Copyright Renewed). Universal-Duches Music Corp. All Rights Reserved. Used by permission. WARNER BROS. PUBLICATION U.S. INC. Miami, FL 33014. 145: "Jambalaya" (On The Bayou) by Hank Williams. © 1952 (Renewed). Acuff-Rose Music, Inc. and Hiriam Music for the USA. All Rights outside USA controlled by Acuff-Rose Music Inc. All Rights reserved. Used By permission. WARNER BROS. PUBLICATIONS U.S. INC. Miami FL 33014. 146: "You Are My Sunshine" words and music by Jimmie Davis and Charles Mitchell, Peer International Corporation, 1940. 148: "Green, Green Grass of Home" by Curly Putnam, © 1965 Sony/ATV Songs LLC. 150: "Summertime" by George Gershwin, Dubose and Dorothy Heyward and Ira Gershwin. © 1935 (Renewed 1962) George Gershwin Music, Ira Gerswhin Music Music and Dubose and Dorothy Heyward Memorial Fund. All rights administered by WB Music Corp. All Rights Reserved. Used by Permission. WARNER BROS. PUBLICATIONS U.S. INC., Miami, Fl. 33014. 152: "Don't Be Cruel" words and music by Otis Blackwell and Elvis Presley. 154: "Downtown" words and music by Anthony Hatch. 156: "Surfin' U.S.A." by Chuck Berry, 1963. Arc Music Corp. 160: "Riendo el río corre" WB MUSIC CORP. Warner Chappell Music Inc. 162: "It's Time." Words and music by Lebo M., John Van Tongeren, and Jay Rifkin. © 1995 Walt Disney Music Company and Wonderland Music Company, Inc. All Rights Reserved. Reprinted by Permission. 165: "Take Time in Life" © 1958 Cooperative Recreation Service, Inc. Delaware, Ohio. Used by permission. 176: "On My Way" lyrics by Brian Crawley, music by Jeanine Tesori, arranged by Michael Rafter, from the musical, *Violet*. 1998 Used by permission. 181: 'Run, Run, Hide" arranged by Linda Twine. This arrangement copyright © 2000 by Hinshaw Music, Inc., Chapel Hill, NC, 27514. International Copyright Secured. All rights reserved. Copying or reproducing this publication in whole or in part violates the Federal Copyright Law. This arrangement is printed with the permission of the publisher. 187: "Rhythm Is Gonna Get You" written by Gloria Estefan and Enrique Garcia. Copyright 1987. Foreign Imported Productions & Publishing, Inc. (BMI) International Rights Secured. All Rights Reserved. Reprinted by permission. 192: "One Moment in Time" words and music by Albert Hammond and John Bettis. All Rights Reserved, Used by Permission. WARNER BROS. PUBLICATIONS U.S. INC. Miami, FL 33014 202: "Worried Man Blues" from Folk Blues by Jerry Silverman. (Macmillan, 1958). 203: "Skye Boat Song," Words by Sir Harold Boulton, Music by Annie MacLeod. All Rights Reserved. Reprinted by permission of Warner Bros. Publications U.S. Inc., Miami, Fl., 33014 210: "Just a Snap-Happy Blues" © 2000 Norma Jean Luckey 216: "A Gift to Share"© 2000 Rollo Dilworth 221: "The Gospel Train" arranged by Shirley W. McRae, 1994 239: "Cantaré, Cantaras" (I Will Sing, You Will Sing) words and music by Albert Hamond & Juan Carlos Calderon. 242: "Who Can Sail?" Finnish Folk Song. Reprinted by permission. Copyright Walton Music Corp. 244: "Ding-Dong Merrily on High," words by G.R. Woodward. arranged by Howard Cable, edited by Henry Leck. Copyright © 1993 by Brassworks

Music, Inc. This arrangement Copyright © 1994 by Brassworks Music, Inc. International Copyright Secured. All Rights Reserved. Reprinted by permission of Canadian Brsss. 251: "Goin to Boston" edited by Henry H. Leck, arranged by Shirley W. McRae. 258: "Under the Same Sun" words and music by Clifford Carter, 1995 264: "One People" Cree words by Noreen Tourangeau and Debbie Nicotine, music and English by Joseph Naytowhow. 1992 267: "I Am But A Small Voice" original words by Odina E. Batnag; English words and music by Roger Whittaker, © 1983 BMG Music Publishing LTD. 270: "The Purple People Eater," words and music by Sheb Wooley. Reprinted by permission. 275: "S'vivon" Hebrew words by L. Kipnis 276: "Winter Song," words and music by Stephen Paulus. Copyright © 1976 by Carl Fischer LLC. International Copyright Secured. All rights reserved. 278: "Caroling, Caroling" Lyric by Wihla Hutson; Music by Alfred Burt. TRO © Copyright 1954(Renewed) Hollis Music, Inc., New York, New York. Used by permission. 282: "Joy of Kwanzaa" © 1999 Reijiro Music 288: "Abraham, Martin and John" by Dick Holler; arranged by Joan R. Hills. © 1968, 1970 Regent Music Coporation. All Rights Reserved. Used by Permission. International Copyright Secured. 294: "I Wish I Knew How It Would Feel To Be Free," music by Billy Taylor and Dick Dalllas. Copyright © 1964 and 1968 by Duane Music Inc. Reprinted with permission. 296: "Eres tu" by Juan Caldreron. All Rights Reserved. Used by Permission. WARNER BROS. PUBLICATIONS U.S. INC., Miami, FL 33014. 300: "Love in Any Language" by John Mohr and John Mays. 308: "Las Mañanitas" words by Lupe Allegria from Children's Songs from Mexico. © Alfred Publishing Co. Inc. Used with permission of the publisher. The editors of Scott, Foresman and Company have made every attempt to verify the source of "Sun Gonna Shine" (p. 143), and "Everybody Loves Saturday Night" (p. 167), but were unable to do so. We believe them to be in the public domain. Every effort has been made to locate all the copyright holders of material used in this book. If any errors or omissions have occurred, corrections will be made.

SONG INDEX

SONG INDEX *continued*

NOTE: These page numbers refer to the actual page in this book. Page numbers for the Pupil Edition appear above the title of each arrangement.